Super San

Recipes

A Complete Cookbook of SF Bay Area Dish
Ideas!

BY

Julia Chiles

OOOOOOOOOOOOOOOOOOOOOOOOOOOOOOOOOOOOOOO

License Notes

No part of this Book can be reproduced in any form or by any means including print, electronic, scanning or photocopying unless prior permission is granted by the author.

All ideas, suggestions and guidelines mentioned here are written for informative purposes. While the author has taken every possible step to ensure accuracy, all readers are advised to follow information at their own risk. The author cannot be held responsible for personal and/or commercial damages in case of misinterpreting and misunderstanding any part of this Book

OOOOOOOOOOOOOOOOOOOOOOOOOOOOOOOOOOOOOO

Thanks for Purchasing My Book! - Here's Your Reward!

Thank you so much for purchasing my book! As a reward for your purchase, you can now receive free books sent to you every week. All you have to do is just subscribe to the list by entering your email address in the box below and I will send you a notification every time I have a free promotion running. The books will absolutely be free with no work at all from you! Who doesn't want free books? No one! *There are free and discounted books every day*, and an email is sent to you 1-2 days beforehand to remind you so you don't miss out. It's that easy! <u>Enter your email now to get started!</u>

cos Sign up now & get your free e-book cos

Refreshing recepies

FIRST NAME: John

YOUR EMAIL: username@domain.com

SIGN UP

http://julia-chiles.subscribemenow.com

OOOOOOOOOOOOOOOOOOOOOOOOOOOOOOOOOOOOOOO

Table of Contents

Introduction

Did you know that the local dishes and restaurants in San Francisco are as famous as their cable cars, winding streets and the iconic Golden Gate Bridge?

Among the regional foods served in San Francisco are bay shrimp, sand dabs, abalone and French sourdough bread.

Can you bring the tastes of the City by the Bay to your dining table? You sure can, with the help of this cookbook.

The San Francisco area has over 300 restaurants that have Michelin stars, which are the most coveted award that a restaurant can receive. The city originated trends like heirloom tomatoes, exotic greens and Asian fusion cuisine.

Even if you don't live anywhere near an ocean, you can find most of the seafood used in San Francisco in your local supermarket. It may be a bit pricy, but if prepared properly, it is SO worth it.

Pick up the freshest produce you can find, so that your dishes have the authentic tastes you're looking for. Read on and discover the tastes of California that you would most like to bring home to your family and guests. There is truly something for everyone in their unique dishes. Turn the page and try some of them soon!

OOOOOOOOOOOOOOOOOOOOOOOOOOOOOOOOOOOOOOO

Breakfast by the Bay will awaken
you with delicious taste. Try one!

ooooooooooooooooooooooooooooooooooooo

1 - Breakfast Pancake Tacos

This is one of the newest breakfast dishes becoming more popular in San Francisco. It is made with all your favorite foods for breakfast, like cheese, eggs and bacon. But the taco "shell" is a pancake!

Serving Size: 8 Servings

Preparation Time: 45 minutes

Ingredients:

- 8 pancakes, premade
- 8 cheddar cheese slices
- 8 strips of bacon, lean
- 1 tbsp. of butter, unsalted
- 6 whisked eggs, large
- Salt, kosher
- Pepper, black, ground
- 1 cup of feta cheese crumbles
- 4 sliced scallions
- Optional, to serve: hot sauce

Instructions:

1. Preheat oven to 375F.

2. Place pancakes on cookie sheets lined with baking paper. Top with cheddar cheese slices.

3. Place bacon on cookie sheet lined with foil. Bake till crisp, about 15-18 minutes. At five minutes left to bake, place pancakes in oven, so cheese can melt.

4. Heat butter in skillet on med. heat. Add whisked eggs. Scramble the eggs for three to four minutes. Then season as desired.

5. Fill pancakes with one scoop each of scrambled eggs and a half-cut piece of lean bacon. Use scallions, feta and hot sauce, if desired, for garnishing. Serve promptly.

OOOOOOOOOOOOOOOOOOOOOOOOOOOOOOOOOOOOOO

2 – Caramel Apple-Style French Toast

Choosing honey crisp apples will be a good start to making this breakfast a success. Crisp, tart apples work best – don't use red delicious or other soft, sweet apples, as they get way too mushy.

Serving Size: 3-6 Servings

Preparation Time: 1 hour 25 minutes + 8 hours refrigeration time

Ingredients:

- 1 loaf of bread, French
- 6 eggs, large
- 1 1/2 cups of milk, low fat
- 1/3 cup of sugar, granulated
- 1 tbsp. of vanilla, pure
- 6 peeled, then cored sliced apples – tart apples work better
- Brown sugar, nutmeg, cinnamon and granulated sugar, as desired

Instructions:

1. Cut the bread in three-inch wide slices. Arrange them in 13x9" pan sprayed with non-stick spray.

2. Beat milk, vanilla, eggs and sugar together in large sized bowl. Pour the mixture over the sliced bread.

3. Arrange the apples atop bread slices. Sprinkle with brown sugar, granulated sugar, cinnamon and nutmeg on top of apples. Cover. Place in the refrigerator overnight.

4. The next morning, bake the pan for an hour in 350F oven till golden brown in color.

5. Top with your choice of caramel topping. Serve.

OOOOOOOOOOOOOOOOOOOOOOOOOOOOOOOOOOOOOO

3 – Chocolate Chip Cappuccino Muffins

This breakfast is super when you're in a hurry, or you can hang around home and savor the taste like you would a cup of great coffee. It has your morning coffee and muffin in one treat.

Serving Size: 14 Muffins

Preparation Time: 40 minutes

Ingredients:

For muffins

- 2 cups of flour, all-purpose
- 1/2 cup of sugar, granulated
- 1/4 cup of brown sugar, packed lightly
- 2 tsp. of baking powder
- 1/2 tsp. of cinnamon, ground
- 1/2 tsp. of salt, kosher
- 1 cup of milk, whole
- 2 tbsp. of espresso powder, instant
- 4 tbsp. of melted butter, unsalted
- 1 egg, large
- 1 tsp. of vanilla, pure
- 1 cup of chocolate chips, mini or regular size

For topping

- 1/4 cup of brown sugar, packed
- 1/4 cup of flour, all-purpose
- 1/4 tsp. of cinnamon, ground
- 1/4 tsp. of salt, kosher
- 4 tbsp. of cold, cubed butter, unsalted

Instructions:

1. Combine the sugar, flour, cinnamon, salt and baking powder.

2. Heat the milk in your microwave for 1 minute. Combine the espresso powder and milk till the granules dissolve. Add egg, vanilla and butter.

3. Stir the wet ingredients into the dry till barely moistened, then add the chocolate chips.

4. Fill a pre-greased, floured pan of muffin cups 2/3 full each.

5. Mix the dry ingredients for streusel mix and cut in the butter. Sprinkle it over the muffins.

6. Bake in 375F oven for 18-20 minutes. Toothpick inserted at middle should come back clean. Allow to cool for five minutes. Remove from the pan and place on a wire rack. Serve.

OOOOOOOOOOOOOOOOOOOOOOOOOOOOOOOOOOOOOO

4 – San Francisco Breakfast Casserole

This casserole is a favorite among Californians, as an overnight prepared dish. It's very easily made. You just throw it together the day before you want to eat it and bake it the next morning.

Serving Size: 12 Servings

Preparation Time: 1 hour 10 minutes

Ingredients:

- 12 frozen and thawed sausage patties, pre-cooked
- 2 or 3 sliced tomatoes
- 2 or 3 sliced avocados
- 12 eggs, large
- 1 cup of milk, 2%
- 1 pound of frozen and thawed hash browns
- 1 cup of shredded cheddar cheese
- 1 tsp. of salt, kosher
- 1/2 tsp. of pepper, ground
- To top: extra cheese shreds

Instructions:

1. Line 13x9" greased pan with the sausage patties.

2. Layer the avocado and tomato slices on top of sausage patties.

3. Beat the milk and eggs in medium bowl.

4. Add and stir remaining ingredients in bowl well.

5. Pour egg hash mixture over sausage, avocados and tomatoes.

6. Bake in 350F oven for 35-40 minutes, till casserole has set well.

7. Remove from oven. Add cheese on top quickly, so it will melt.

8. Serve along with sour cream, salsa or diced tomatoes, as desired.

OOOOOOOOOOOOOOOOOOOOOOOOOOOOOOOOOOOOOOO

5 – Yogurt with Figs

One of the best things about living in California is ready access to fresh ingredients and produce. Many dishes, like this one, are made easy because of easily-found veggies and fruits.

Serving Size: 1 Serving

Preparation Time: 5-7 minutes

Ingredients:

- 1 cup of yogurt, plain
- 2 figs, fresh
- 1/4 cup of blackberries, fresh
- 2 tbsp. of pistachios, chopped
- 1 tbsp. of honey, + extra if desired

Instructions:

1. Spoon the yogurt into small sized bowl.

2. Next, half-slice the figs lengthways. Add to bowl. Add pistachios and blackberries.

3. Drizzle over the top with the honey. Serve.

oooooooooooooooooooooooooooooooooooooo

San Francisco is SO diverse, you'll find many kinds of recipes for lunch, dinner, side dishes and appetizers... try one soon!

ooooooooooooooooooooooooooooooooooooooooooo

6 – Salmon Edamame Noodles

Edamame beans and salmon pair so well together. The noodles made with edamame are healthy and light, and, unlike typical pasta noodles, they offer you protein.

Serving Size: 2 Servings

Preparation Time: 25 minutes

Ingredients:

- 1 box of spaghetti, edamame
- 2 fillets, salmon
- Oil, olive
- Salt, kosher, as desired
- Pepper, ground, as desired

Instructions:

1. Cook noodles using instructions on the package. Drain them and set them aside.

2. Heat oil in skillet. Cook salmon for several minutes per side till it flakes easily using a fork.

3. Season salmon as desired.

4. Toss spaghetti with oil. Serve with salmon.

OOOOOOOOOOOOOOOOOOOOOOOOOOOOOOOOOOOOOOOO

7 - Avocado Shrimp Salad

This is a refreshing salad that features the ever-popular avocado. Once people have had avocados, they often include it in many dishes, like this one.

Serving Size: 4 Servings

Preparation Time: 35 minutes

Ingredients:

- 1/4 cup of pumpkin seeds, raw
- 1/4 cup + 1 tbsp. of oil, olive
- 2 tbsp. of lime juice, fresh
- 1 sliced shallot, small
- 1/4 cup of cilantro, chopped
- 1 grapefruit, large
- 1 wedge-cut avocado
- Salt, kosher
- Pepper, fresh ground
- 3/4 lb. of shrimp, large, shelled, de-veined
- 1 bite-size torn head Boston lettuce

Instructions:

1. Preheat oven to 400F.

2. Spread pumpkin seeds on small cookie sheet. Bake them for three minutes, till they are toasted lightly. Transfer to plate. Allow them to cool.

3. Combine 3 tbsp. oil, cilantro, shallot and lime juice in large sized bowl.

4. Peel grapefruit and remove pith. Cut between membranes over bowl, releasing the sections in the bowl. Squeeze membrane juice into bowl and discard membranes.

5. Fold avocado in gently. Season as desired.

6. Heat remaining 2 tsp. oil in medium sized skillet till it shimmers. Add shrimp and season as desired. Cook on med. heat and toss shrimp till they become pink and curled.

7. Arrange lettuce on platter. Lift avocado and grapefruit from citrus dressing with slotted spoon. Spread gently on lettuce. Add shrimp to vinaigrette dressing. Toss and coat them well.

8. Arrange shrimp over salad. Drizzle the rest of the citrus dressing over the top. Scatter with pumpkin seeds. Serve promptly.

OOOOOOOOOOOOOOOOOOOOOOOOOOOOOOOOOOOOOO

8 - Haricots Verts Hazelnuts

A salad made with haricots verts gets a boost in taste and texture with a creamy, tomato-spiked dressing and fresh hazel nuts. If you don't have green hazel nuts in your area, you can use blanched, ripe hazel nuts.

Serving Size: 4 Servings

Preparation Time: 35 minutes

Ingredients:

- Salt, kosher
- 1 pound of haricots verts, trimmed (can substitute regular green beans)
- 1/2 cup of hazelnuts, green, with skins removed
- 3/4 cup of crème fraiche
- 1 tbsp. of vinegar, red-wine
- Pepper, black, ground
- 2 de-seeded, diced tomatoes, medium
- 3 cups of baby greens, mixed
- 3 fresh basil leaves

Instructions:

1. Bring pot of lightly salted water to boil on high heat. Add the haricots verts or regular green beans. Cook till they are tender, or five to eight minutes. Drain the beans and refresh them in cold, filtered water. Wrap them in a kitchen towel and set them aside.

2. Chop hazelnuts coarsely. Set them aside.

3. To prepare the dressing, place the crème fraîche in medium sized bowl. Whisk in the vinegar, kosher salt ground pepper.

4. Add tomatoes. Gently stir. Set them aside for 10-12 minutes, so the tomatoes can add color and flavor to the dressing.

5. For salad assembly, toss the greens in medium sized bowl with 2 tbsp. of dressing. Divide evenly on four individual plates. Transfer haricots verts to the bowl and add 1/2 cup +/- of the dressing. Toss and coat well.

6. Arrange the haricots verts atop greens. Spoon remainder of dressing over the individual salads. Be sure they all get several diced tomatoes. Sprinkle with the hazelnuts. Use basil leaves to garnish. Serve.

OOOOOOOOOOOOOOOOOOOOOOOOOOOOOOOOOOOOOOOO

9 – Mulligatawny Soup

This soup is one of the main attractions at a local restaurant in San Francisco and is a twist on the cuisine of Sri Lanka. Their take on the concept of mulligatawny soup will warm you up on those sometimes-chilly days in San Francisco.

Serving Size: 10-12 Servings

Preparation Time: 50 minutes

Ingredients:

- 5 cloves of garlic, medium-sized
- 2 red onions, large
- 3 or 4 peeled carrots, medium
- 1 peeled, cored apple
- 1 peeled potato, large
- 1 de-stemmed Serrano pepper, fresh
- 1" knob of ginger, fresh
- 1" piece of turmeric, fresh
- 1 cup of washed and rinsed lentils, red
- 2 x 14-ounce cans of coconut milk, full-fat
- Curry spice mixture – see individual spices below
- Salt, kosher, as desired
- The curry spices
- 1 tsp. of peppercorns, black
- 1 tsp. each of mustard seeds, fennel seeds, cumin seeds
- 1 tsp. each of cinnamon sticks, turmeric, whole cardamom pods and curry leaves

Instructions:

1. Dice turmeric, ginger, pepper, potato, apple, carrots, onions and garlic in 3/4-inch cubes.

2. Grind cumin seeds, fennel, mustard and peppercorns into a powder.

3. Coat bottom of large pot with slick of oil. Heat on med-high.

4. Add cinnamon sticks, curry leaves and cardamom pods. Cook while stirring for one to two minutes.

5. Add diced veggies and remaining spices. Stir again till spices have been distributed evenly in vegetables. Cook for several minutes. Vegetables should be starting to become brown.

6. Add the lentils. Stir and add water to cover all ingredients in pot. Cover. Cook till lentils and vegetables become tender.

7. Add coconut milk. Bring to boil.

8. Allow the soup to cool. Then blend and strain it and serve.

OOOOOOOOOOOOOOOOOOOOOOOOOOOOOOOOOOOOO

10 – Goat Cheese Tomato Confit

Rather than finishing this meal with butter, this recipe features goat cheese. The gentle heat turns it creamy. It's especially tasty with sourdough bread.

Serving Size: 8 Servings

Preparation Time: 1 hour 40 minutes

Ingredients:

- 2 lbs. of quartered, de-seeded tomatoes, Roma if available
- 2/3 oz. of basil sprigs
- 3 sliced garlic cloves
- 1 bunch of thyme sprigs, fresh
- 2 tbsp. of oil, olive, as desired
- Salt, kosher
- Pepper, black, as desired
- 1 x 4-oz. log of sliced goat cheese
- 3 tbsp. of pesto, as desired

Instructions:

1. Preheat the oven to 350F.

2. Lay the tomatoes with the skin side facing down on rimmed cookie sheet. Layer the garlic, basil and thyme on the top.

3. Drizzle the oil on tomatoes and season as desired.

4. Bake at 350F till soft, 45 minutes to an hour. Cool for 20 minutes or more.

5. Discard thyme and basil sprigs. Peel the tomatoes. Transfer them to serving dish. Put the goat cheese on the top. Dollop a tsp. of pesto over slices of goat cheese.

6. Bake at 350F till cheese becomes soft and starts browning. Remove from oven. Serve.

OOOOOOOOOOOOOOOOOOOOOOOOOOOOOOOOOOOOOOOO

11 – Mission District Fried Chicken

This dish takes its name from the Mission District in San Francisco, where the restaurant whose chef created it is located. The use of red chili flakes and Madras curry powder adds a lot of kick!

Serving Size: 4 Servings

Preparation Time: 25 minutes

Ingredients:

- 3 tbsp. + 1 tsp. of curry powder
- 1 tsp. of garlic powder
- 1 pinch sugar, granulated
- 1/8 tsp. of chili flakes, red
- 1 x 3-lb. chicken, cut in eight pieces
- 3 tsp. of salt, kosher + extra to season
- 4 cups of oil, grapeseed, + extra as needed
- 2 cups of flour, all-purpose
- 1 tsp. of pepper, black, ground
- 3 cups of buttermilk
- 3 tbsp. of sesame seeds

Instructions:

1. Combine 3 tbsp. of curry powder with chili flakes, garlic powder and sugar. Set mixture aside.

2. To season chicken, salt all pieces liberally. Rub curry mix lightly over pieces.

3. Combine flour with sesame seeds, pepper, 1 tbsp. curry powder and 1 tsp. salt. Set the mixture aside.

4. Preheat oil in heavy skillet at 300F.

5. Combine buttermilk and 1 tsp. salt in large sized bowl. As oil warms gently, dip curried pieces of chicken in buttermilk. Press into flour mixture and cover each piece well. Place them on plate. Repeat till all chicken pieces are breaded.

6. Place pieces of chicken with skin side facing down in skillet. Don't overcrowd pan.

7. Cook the chicken on the first side for seven to eight minutes. Turn the pieces gently over. Cook till done. Continue till you have cooked all chicken pieces. Add extra oil if you need to. Maintain 300F oil, so chicken will cook more evenly.

8. Place fried chicken on sheet pan on rack. Place in 200F oven till time for serving. When all the pieces are done, serve.

OOOOOOOOOOOOOOOOOOOOOOOOOOOOOOOOOOOOOO

12 - Salmon Gravlax

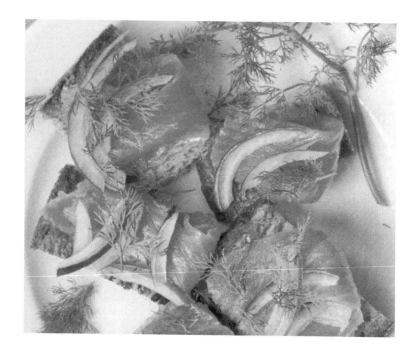

You can make salmon gravlax easily in your home. It Makes an enjoyable project that requires little effort - and it will impress even your hardest-to-please diners.

Serving Size: 4 Servings

Preparation Time: 6 hours 25 minutes + 54 hours refrigerator time

Ingredients:

- 1/4 cup of salt, kosher
- 1/4 cup of sugar, granulated
- 1 pinch of pepper, cayenne
- 1 x 8-oz. tail section of salmon, skin-on
- 1 beet, small

Instructions:

1. Stir the cayenne, salt and sugar together in medium bowl.

2. Line dish with kitchen towel or cheese cloth. Sprinkle 1/3 of sugar/salt mixture on bottom.

3. Place salmon with the skin facing down in bowl. Grate beet over salmon. Evenly spread and cover salmon. Sprinkle the rest of the sugar/salt mixture over the top.

4. Fold the towel over salmon. Cover top using cling wrap. Wrap brick in foil. Place atop salmon. Allow to cure in refrigerator till salmon feels firm to touch and appears translucent when you slice it. This usually takes 36 hours or so.

5. Transfer the salmon to plate lined with paper towels. Scrape off grated beet. Then cover with cling wrap. Place back in refrigerator for 18 hours more or so.

6. Slice salmon and serve.

OOOOOOOOOOOOOOOOOOOOOOOOOOOOOOOOOOOOOOOO

13 - Roasted Eggplant Yogurt

When it's eggplant season, every size, variety and color is everywhere in the local vegetable stands. This dish includes eggplant with a wonderful sauce made from Greek yogurt.

Serving Size: 4 Servings

Preparation Time: 1 hour 10 minutes

Ingredients:

For eggplant

- 6 eggplants
- 1/2 cup of oil, olive
- Salt, kosher
- Pepper, black, ground

For savory yogurt

- 2 tbsp. of oil, olive
- 1 cup of organic yogurt, plain
- 1 tbsp. of lemon juice, fresh
- 1 minced garlic clove
- Salt, kosher
- Optional for garnishing: cilantro

Instructions:

1. Slice eggplants into halves. Cut cross-hatch in top, not completely through to skin. Brush halves with oil. Sprinkle with kosher salt and ground pepper. Place on cookie sheet.

2. Roast at 400F for 1/2 hour. Flesh should be soft to touch. Allow them to completely cool.

3. Stir 1 pinch salt, 1 minced garlic clove, 1 tbsp. lemon juice, 2 tbsp. oil and 1 cup yogurt together. Spoon some on each eggplant. Garnish them with fresh herbs. Serve.

OOOOOOOOOOOOOOOOOOOOOOOOOOOOOOOOOOOOOO

14 – Cashew, Watermelon Feta Salad

The dish in this recipe was inspired by a salad served in a café in San Francisco. This is a home-style version, which is still a wonderful combination of crunchy, creamy, juicy, salty and sweet.

Serving Size: 8 Servings

Preparation Time: 20 minutes

Ingredients:

- 1 small watermelon, seedless, ripe
- 1 head of lettuce, Boston or Bibb
- 4 oz. of feta cheese
- 1/2 cup of cashews, toasted
- 1/4 cup of vinegar, rice
- 1/4 cup of oil, olive
- Salt, kosher, as desired
- Pepper, ground, as desired
- Optional: basil leaves or fresh mint

Instructions:

1. Slice watermelon in half. Scoop melon out with melon baller and place in bowl.

2. Separate lettuce leaves. Arrange the leaves to resemble cups in one layer on platter. Place the melon balls on lettuce and crumble feta over salad. Top with cashews.

3. Whisk the kosher salt, ground pepper, oil and vinegar together and drizzle mixture over salad. Use basil leaves or mint to garnish. Serve.

OOOOOOOOOOOOOOOOOOOOOOOOOOOOOOOOOOOOOOO

15 – Asparagus Leek Soup

This soup is a fresh, light dish that brings the taste of spring into your home. The lemon brightens the dish and the soup can be served as a starter course or light meal.

Serving Size: 4 Servings

Preparation Time: 55 minutes

Ingredients:

- 4 cups of broth, vegetable
- 1 lb. of trimmed, chopped asparagus, with woody ends reserved
- 3 tbsp. of oil, olive
- 4 minced garlic cloves
- Light green white parts of 3 leeks, small
- 2 tbsp. of flour, all-purpose
- 1 1/2 tsp. of salt, kosher
- 1/2 tsp. of pepper, ground
- 1/4 cup of lemon juice, fresh
- Crème fraîche

Instructions:

1. Place woody ends of asparagus in small sized sauce pan. Pour in broth. Simmer for 12-15 minutes, infusing broth with flavor of asparagus.

2. Heat oil in large sized pot. Add leeks and garlic. Sauté on med. heat for 8-10 minutes. Stir continuously while adding flour for a couple minutes, making a roux.

3. Remove woody asparagus stems from broth. Discard. Pour broth in large pot with garlic and leeks. Add raw asparagus. Simmer for 8-10 minutes, till asparagus is tender and bright green.

4. Remove pot from heat. Use blender to puree the mixture in small sized batches till the mixture has a smooth texture.

5. Season as desired. Add and stir lemon juice. Top with crème fraîche. Serve.

OOOOOOOOOOOOOOOOOOOOOOOOOOOOOOOOOOOOOO

16 - Ramblas Cranberry Bean Ragout

Ramblas is the restaurant where this wonderful dish was conceived. It's a great side that features currants, citrus and beans stewed with corn.

Serving Size: 4 Servings

Preparation Time: 1 hour 10 minutes

Ingredients:

- 2 tbsp. of oil, olive
- 2 sliced garlic cloves
- 1 cup of stock, chicken, as needed
- 1 cup of cranberry beans, shelled
- 1 cup of corn kernels
- 1/4 cup of diced tomatoes, ripe
- 2 tbsp. of currants, dried
- 1 tbsp. of lemon zest, fresh, + extra for garnishing
- Salt, kosher, as desired
- Pepper, ground, as desired
- 2 tbsp. of chopped oregano, fresh

Instructions:

1. Heat the oil in large skillet on med. heat. Cook the sliced garlic till toasted lightly.

2. Pour 1/2 cup of stock over garlic. Add the lemon zest, currants, tomatoes, corn and cranberry beans. Season as desired. Stir well. Sprinkle top with a pinch of oregano.

3. Bring mixture to simmer. Then reduce the heat to med-low. Add a splash more stock. Cook at simmer. Stir occasionally. Add additional broth if you need it, if the mixture starts to look dry, till beans are fully tender.

4. Stir the rest of the oregano into bean and corn mixture. Transfer to plate. Use lemon zest to garnish and serve.

OOOOOOOOOOOOOOOOOOOOOOOOOOOOOOOOOOOOO

17 - Oysters Pickled Ginger

This dish is often served with sushi, but the pickled ginger makes it a wonderful match for oysters, too. The pickled ginger and diced shallots make an easy garnish.

Serving Size: 6-8 Servings

Preparation Time: 25 minutes + 1/2 hour freezer time

Ingredients:

- 3 tbsp. of shallots, minced
- 3 tbsp. of ginger, pickled
- 2 tbsp. of lime juice, fresh
- 2 tbsp. of vinegar, rice wine
- 1 tbsp. of sake
- Pepper, black, cracked
- Optional: cilantro blossoms to garnish
- 24 oysters, fresh

Instructions:

1. Dice ginger and shallot finely. Add to remainder of ingredients in small sized freezer-safe plate or dish. Grind a bit of pepper on the top.

2. Freeze for 20 minutes to a half-hour. Once it has frozen, use a fork to scrape and loosen mixture, forming crystals.

3. Shuck oysters. Place atop tray of crushed ice. Place granita in small sized bowl. Garnish oysters with cilantro blossoms. Serve with oysters.

OOOOOOOOOOOOOOOOOOOOOOOOOOOOOOOOOOOOOOO

18 – Mexi-Cali Shrimp Cocktail

Mexican-style food like burritos and tacos can be found almost anywhere in the U.S. today. But Mexi-Cali shrimp cocktails are catching on, too, especially in the bay area. Taste one and you'll know why.

Serving Size: 4 Servings

Preparation Time: 1 1/2 hours + 2 to 3 hours refrigerator time

Ingredients:

- 1 cup of clam juice
- 1/4 tsp. of oregano, dried
- 1 lb. of peeled, de-veined shrimp, large
- 1 1/4 cups of ripe tomatoes, peeled, de-seeded and diced
- 1 cup of English cucumber, diced
- 1/2 cup of celery, diced
- 1/2 cup of diced onion, red
- 2 tbsp. of de-seeded, diced peppers, jalapeno
- 1/2 cup of catsup
- 2 fresh limes, juice only
- 2 tbsp. of cilantro, chopped + extra for garnishing
- Hot sauce, Mexican style, as desired
- 1 cubed avocado, large

Instructions:

1. Place oregano and clam juice in sauce pan. Bring to boil on med-high. Add the shrimp. Stir only till shrimp become pink and are not yet cooked all the way through. This takes two minutes, more or less.

2. Transfer the shrimp to bowl. Reserve the liquid. Allow shrimp to cool down to room temperature.

3. Next, place jalapenos, onions, celery, cucumbers and tomatoes in medium bowl. Add the catsup, along with hot sauce (if desired), cilantro, lime juice and cooking liquid from shrimp. Mix gently till ingredients are blended well.

4. Chop the shrimp into small pieces. Leave several whole to use as a garnish. Stir the chopped pieces in veggie mixture.

5. Wrap the bowl with cling wrap. Place the reserved shrimp in bowl and wrap with cling wrap, as well. Refrigerate the reserved shrimp and shrimp cocktail till chilled well.

6. Add and stir avocado pieces. Transfer mixture to glass bowls. Top with the whole shrimp reserved earlier and add a few cilantro leaves to each. Serve.

OOOOOOOOOOOOOOOOOOOOOOOOOOOOOOOOOOOOOOOO

19 - Tomato Salad Yogurt Dressing

Cold, fresh tomatoes are such a brilliant contrast to the ones usually served only slightly cool in salads. In this recipe, they are chilled on plates in your refrigerator before you finish up the entire salad, with the herbs and dressing.

Serving Size: 4 Servings

Preparation Time: 35 minutes

Ingredients:

For salad

- 1 pound +/- of tomatoes, fresh
- 1 handful of dill leaves, fresh
- Salt, sea
- 1 tbsp. of peppercorns, pink
- Oil, olive

For dressing

- 1 cup yogurt
- 2 tbsp. of oil, olive
- 1 tbsp. lemon juice, fresh
- 1 minced garlic clove
- 2 to 3 tbsp. of milk, whole
- Salt, sea

Instructions:

1. Slice larger tomatoes. Wedge-cut smaller tomatoes. Arrange tomatoes on serving plate. Place in fridge for 1/2 hour or longer.

2. Stir yogurt ingredients except milk and salt together in small sized bowl. Add 1 tbsp. of milk after another, stirring together so the dressing is thin enough to spoon over salad.

3. Remove tomatoes from fridge. Spoon a few splashes of dressing over tomatoes. Add peppercorns and dill. Sprinkle with sea salt. Drizzle entire salad with oil. Serve promptly.

OOOOOOOOOOOOOOOOOOOOOOOOOOOOOOOOOOOOOOO

20 - San Francisco Pork Chops

These tender pork chops are served in a delectable sauce. They taste wonderful when you serve them over thin spaghetti or noodles. The presentation is beautiful, too.

Serving Size: 4 Servings

Preparation Time: 1 hour 10 minutes

Ingredients:

- 1 tbsp. of oil, vegetable
- 4 trimmed pork chops, boneless, 3/4" thick
- 1 minced garlic clove
- 1/4 cup of broth, beef
- 1/4 cup of soy sauce, reduced sodium
- 2 tbsp. of sugar, brown
- 2 tsp. of oil, vegetable
- 1/4 tsp. of pepper flakes, red
- 2 tsp. of corn starch
- 2 tsp. of water, filtered

Instructions:

1. Heat 1 tbsp. of oil in skillet on med. heat. Then brown the pork chops in the hot oil. It should take four or five minutes for each side. Remove the chops to plate and reserve the oil in the skillet.

2. Stir while cooking cloves of garlic in the reserved drippings till they become fragrant. Whisk the broth, soy sauce, 2 tsp. oil, pepper flakes and brown sugar in a bowl. Mix to dissolve the brown sugar.

3. Return chops to the skillet. Add soy sauce mixture on top. Bring sauce to boil and cover the skillet. Reduce the heat down to low and simmer the chops till they are tender. Turn once while cooking.

4. Transfer pork chops to serving platter. Then whisk water and corn starch in bowl till they have a smooth texture. Stir this into the juices in the pan. Simmer till it thickens. Pour the sauce over the chops and serve.

OOOOOOOOOOOOOOOOOOOOOOOOOOOOOOOOOOOOO

21 - Dungeness Crab Cakes

A trip to the restaurants near the Golden Gate Bridge will reveal the tempting taste of Dungeness crab cakes, but you can make them at home, too. Purchase freshly cleaned and steamed crabs if you'll be preparing them in your own kitchen.

Serving Size: 14 crab cakes

Preparation Time: 35 minutes

Ingredients:

- 1 egg, large
- 2 tbsp. of mayonnaise, light
- 1/2 tbsp. of lemon juice, fresh
- 1/2 tsp. of mustard, Dijon
- 1 tbsp. each of chopped parsley, chervil and dill
- 1 tbsp. of sliced chives
- 1/2 tsp. of seasoning, Old Bay
- 1/2 tsp. of salt, sea
- 1 cup of panko bread crumbs
- 8 to 10 oz. of crab meat, cracked, cleaned
- Oil, olive
- Lemon wedges, to serve

Instructions:

1. Whisk the egg in medium bowl. Add and whisk nine next ingredients after egg.

2. Add 1/4 cup of panko bread crumbs to egg mixture. Once you combine them well, fold in crab gently. Put the rest of the panko on plate, for dredging.

3. Form crab patties from crab mixture. They should be about 1 1/2" x 3/4" and you'll have 14 +/- total patties. Dredge them in the panko bread crumbs. Refrigerate for an hour or more so they can firm up.

4. Heat 1-2 tbsp. oil in non-stick skillet, coating the bottom of it. When oil gets hot, add crab cakes. Turn after two or three minutes, when they are a golden brown in color.

5. Wipe skillet with paper towels between each batch, so panko bread crumbs will not burn. Serve crab cakes with the wedges of fresh lemon.

OOOOOOOOOOOOOOOOOOOOOOOOOOOOOOOOOOOOOOO

22 - San Francisco Bay Cioppino

This seafood stew harkens back to the childhood of people who grew up in the San Francisco area. It's red, rich tasting and quite messy, and often served for New Year's celebrations in California.

Serving Size: 8 Servings

Preparation Time: 2 hours 25 minutes

Ingredients:

- 2 tbsp. of oil, olive
- 1 chopped onion, large
- 3 crushed garlic cloves, +/- as desired
- 2 x 28-oz. cans of tomatoes in juice, diced
- 1/2 cup of white wine, dry
- 1/4 cup of chopped parsley, fresh
- 1/2 tsp. of basil, dried
- 2 tsp. of salt, sea
- 1/2 tsp. of cracked pepper, black
- 1 lb. of scallops
- 1 bay leaf
- 24 clams, littleneck
- 1 1/2 lbs. of crab legs
- 1 lb. of large, unpeeled shrimp, fresh

Instructions:

1. Heat the oil in large and heavy pot on med-high. Add garlic and onion. Stir frequently while cooking, till they are soft.

2. Add wine and tomatoes. Season with bay leaf, sea salt, ground pepper, basil and parsley. Reduce the heat down to med-low. Simmer till liquid has been almost completely reduced. This usually takes an hour or so.

3. Add the shrimp, crab legs, clams and scallops to pot. Cover. Cook on med. heat till the clams have opened. Scoop desired portions into large, individual bowls. Serve.

OOOOOOOOOOOOOOOOOOOOOOOOOOOOOOOOOOOOOOOOO

23 - Pork Tacos Peach Relish

When you pair peaches with spicy chilies, this dish brings some cooling effect to the spicy, hot flavors of the recipe. It works especially well with meats that have been braised and grilled.

Serving Size: 6 Servings

Preparation Time: 5 1/4 hours

Ingredients:

For pork:

- 4 lbs. of halved pork shoulder, boneless
- 1 tbsp. of salt, kosher
- 1/2 tbsp. of pepper, ground
- 1/2 tbsp. of chili flakes, red
- 2 tbsp. of oil, canola
- 3 cups of water, filtered

For relish

- 1/2 cup of large, slivered shallots
- 2 halved, slivered chilies, Fresno
- 1/2 cup of fennel, shaved
- 1 fresh lemon, juice only
- 1 1/2 cups of sliced peaches
- 1 small handful of chopped cilantro
- To serve: tortillas, warmed

Instructions:

1. Preheat the oven to 300F.

2. Combine kosher salt, ground pepper and chili flakes in small sized bowl. Coat pieces of the pork with mixture. Allow them to sit out at room temp. for 1/2 hour or so.

3. Add oil to large, oven-safe pot. Heat till nearly smoking. Then brown pork, 1 half after the other, till all sides have turned deeply brown.

4. Place all pork back in same large pot. Add water till it is 1/2 way up meat sides. Bring to simmer. Cover with a lid.

5. Place in oven. Cook for five to six hours. Flip meat over when halfway done. When fully cooked, meat will be fall-apart tender, pulling off easily with fork.

6. Remove meat from oven. Allow it to rest for 1/2 hour.

7. To prepare relish, combine lemon juice, fennel, chilies and shallots in medium sized bowl. Add pinch of kosher salt.

8. Quarter-cut peaches. Slice them thinly and add to shallots mixture. Add and mix cilantro. Season as desired.

9. Break pork apart with fork. Remove fat. Transfer to serving platter.

10. Serve braised pork peach relish on warm tortillas.

OOOOOOOOOOOOOOOOOOOOOOOOOOOOOOOOOOOOOOOO

24 – Garlic Noodles

These noodles are tantalizingly delicious but deceptively easy to prepare. They were first served in the 1970's, in a San Francisco restaurant, Thanh Long. They taste especially wonderful with Dungeness crab.

Serving Size: 2 Servings

Preparation Time: 40 minutes

Ingredients:

For sauce:

- 2 tbsp. of soy sauce, reduced sodium
- 1 tbsp. of oyster sauce
- 2 tsp. of Worcestershire sauce, low sodium
- 2 tsp. of fish sauce, prepared
- 1/4 tsp. of oil, sesame
- 1 pinch of pepper, cayenne

For noodles:

- 8 minced garlic cloves
- 4 tbsp. of butter, unsalted
- 1/4 cup of cheese, Parmigiano-Reggiano, grated finely
- 1 tbsp. of green onion, chopped, +/- as desired
- 6 oz. of spaghetti, pre-cooked using instructions on package
- A pinch of pepper flakes, red

Instructions:

1. Stir the cayenne pepper, sesame oil, fish sauce, Worcestershire sauce, oyster sauce and soy sauce in small sized bowl. This will be your sauce.

2. Place the sauce close to the stove. Use individual bowls for each of green onions, Parmigiano-Reggiano cheese, butter and garlic. Be sure it's easy to reach the bowls from the stove.

3. Melt the butter in skillet on med. heat. Add the garlic. Stir while cooking only till garlic becomes fragrant, usually a minute or so. Stir in sauce and turn off burner.

4. Transfer the spaghetti into sauce with tongs. Add a bit of water if desired. Toss till coated well. Add Parmesan cheese. Transfer noodles to plates. Use green onions and red pepper flakes to garnish. Serve.

OOOOOOOOOOOOOOOOOOOOOOOOOOOOOOOOOOOOOOOO

25 - Sausage Broccoli Rabe Tartine

Many people confuse broccoli rabe with regular broccoli, but broccoli rabe has more bite to it. It's related to mustard greens and turnips, and you'll especially enjoy serving the willowy stems, leafy bits and flowery parts.

Serving Size: 4 Servings

Preparation Time: 25 minutes

Ingredients:

- 1/2 lb. of broccoli rabe
- 1/2 lb. of sausage links with removed casings
- 1 handful of torn mushrooms
- Oil, olive
- 1 loaf of bread, crusty
- 12 oz. of ricotta, sheep's milk
- Optional: chili flakes, red

Instructions:

1. Preheat the oven for broiling.

2. Trim bottom 1" of broccoli rabe. Halve-cut the large sized stalks lengthways.

3. Sauté mushrooms and sausage in large sized skillet till sausage is cooked and has crumbled. Set the mixture aside.

4. Turn heat on high. Add drizzle of oil. Sauté the broccoli rabe till greens have wilted and stems and flowers have softened. Add mushrooms and sausage back in skillet, so the flavors will combine. Season as desired.

5. Slice bread in thick slices. Drizzle them with the olive oil. Broil till browned and turn once while cooking. Both sides should be crisp.

6. Spread toast with ricotta. Top with broccoli rabe mixture. Finish with pinch of chili flakes, as desired and serve.

OOOOOOOOOOOOOOOOOOOOOOOOOOOOOOOOOOOOOO

They make some of THE best tasting desserts in San Francisco... Here are a few of the tastiest...

ooooooooooooooooooooooooooooooooooooooooooo

26 – Cream Cheese Apple Pie

These rustic pies stand out on any dessert table. The cream cheese gives them a tang that balances the tart, sweet flavors of baked apples. They are a hit at parties and get-togethers of most any kind.

Serving Size: 12 Servings

Preparation Time: 1 1/2 hour

Ingredients:

- 2-crust pie dough, store bought
- 4 peeled, then cored and sliced apples, large
- 1/2 cup of sugar, granulated
- 2 tbsp. of corn starch
- 2 tsp. of lemon juice, fresh
- 1 tsp. of cinnamon, ground
- 1/4 tsp. of nutmeg, ground
- 1/4 tsp. of salt, kosher
- 12 oz. of softened cream cheese
- 2 tbsp. of sugar, granulated
- 2 tsp. of vanilla, pure
- For washing: 1 egg, large
- Sugar, raw, to finish

Instructions:

1. Toss corn starch, apples, lemon juice, 1/2 cup of granulated sugar, kosher salt, cinnamon and nutmeg in large sized bowl. Set it aside.

2. Mix vanilla, cream cheese and 2 tbsp. of granulated sugar till you have a smooth texture.

3. Divide pie dough in two crusts. Flour a work surface. Roll each crust to a diameter of 12" or so.

4. Divide cream cheese and vanilla mixture into two portions. Evenly spread on dough. Leave a border on the outside of 1/2" or so.

5. Start at outside and arrange apple slices on top of the cream cheese and vanilla mixture. Leave 1" border around outside. Discard the rest of the liquid.

6. Fold uncovered dough over apples and overlap them. Leave a small area of the middle fruit exposed.

7. Next, place the galettes you just formed on a cookie sheet lined with baking paper.

8. Whisk the egg in small sized bowl. Brush over exposed dough using generous egg coating. Sprinkle galettes with sugar.

9. Bake galettes in 400F oven for 35-45 minutes, till crust is a golden brown color. Serve while warm.

OOOOOOOOOOOOOOOOOOOOOOOOOOOOOOOOOOOOOOO

27 - Lemon Pistachio Cheesecake Bites

These little cheesecakes are easy to make, and their taste isn't too tangy OR too sweet. They will satisfy your appetite without killing a calorie counter's day. Four mini cakes are still fewer calories than one slice of a regular cheesecake.

Serving Size: 6-8 Servings

Preparation Time: 1 hour 5 minutes + 8-24 hours refrigeration time

Ingredients:

For the crust

- 1/2 cup of finely ground pistachio nuts, unsalted
- 1/2 cup of crumbled graham crackers
- 3 tbsp. of sugar, granulated
- 3 tbsp. of melted butter, unsalted

For the cheesecake

- 1 egg, large
- 1 cup of cream cheese, whipped
- 1/4 cup of sugar, granulated
- 1 tsp. of vanilla extract, pure
- 2 tsp. of lemon zest, fresh
- 24 tsp. of lemon curd

Instructions:

1. Preheat the oven to 375F. Spray 24 cups of mini muffin pan with non-stick spray.

2. To prepare the crust, mix the sugar, nuts and crumbled graham crackers together. Add the melted butter. Mix well.

3. Use a little less than 1 tbsp. of the crust mixture in each mini muffin cup. Press down a bit so mixture stays firmly at the bottom of cups. Set the pan aside.

4. Combine the cheesecake ingredients in small sized bowl. Mix till you have a smooth consistency.

5. Pour a bit less than 1 tbsp. of the cheesecake mixture into mini muffin cups, on top of the crust mixture. Place in oven and bake for 15-18 minutes. The mixture will usually puff and may crack.

6. Once cheesecake mini's have brown slightly around the edges, test them by pressing gently on top. If that does not leave any mark, remove the pan from oven. Let the mini cakes cool. Expect the center to sink a bit.

7. Top with a tsp. of lemon curd on each mini cheesecake. Serve.

OOOOOOOOOOOOOOOOOOOOOOOOOOOOOOOOOOOOOOOO

28 - Light Sweet Blackberry Scones

If you think that scones are always tasteless and dry, these will come as a most pleasant surprise. They are different from regular scones, and are sweet, moist and fluffy.

Serving Size: 8 Servings

Preparation Time: 35 minutes

Ingredients:

- 2 cups of flour, white
- 3 tbsp. of sugar, granulated
- 1 1/2 tsp. of baking powder
- 1 stick of softened butter, unsalted
- 3/4 cup of milk, whole
- 1/3 cup of blackberries – or sub a favorite fruit of your own
- Optional: 1/3 cup of chocolate chips, white
- Sugar, raw

Instructions:

1. Preheat the oven to 375F.

2. Mix the butter, baking powder, sugar and flour in electric mixer set on low, till all are combined well. It should look like oatmeal.

3. Add the milk. Mix till well-blended. Fold in the berries and chocolate chips, as desired.

4. Turn the dough out on floured surface. Form a round with a thickness of 1-inch. Generously sprinkle with the raw sugar.

5. Slice into eight wedges. Place them on a cookie sheet. Bake for 15-20 minutes, till they turn a golden brown in color. Serve.

ooooooooooooooooooooooooooooooooooooo

29 - SF Brandy, Oatmeal Pear Cookies

These delectable cookies are a bit healthier than typical cookies. The pear puree replaces butter. You can also amp up the flavor if you soak the raisins in brandy.

Serving Size: 36 cookies +/-

Preparation Time: 1 1/4 hour

Ingredients:

- 3/4 cup packed brown sugar
- 1 cup raisins, jumbo if available
- 1/4 cup brandy
- 1 1/2 cup filtered water, hot
- 1 1/2 cup flour, all-purpose
- 1 tsp. of baking soda
- 2 eggs, large
- 1 tsp. ground cinnamon
- 1/2 tsp. salt, kosher
- 1 stick softened butter, unsalted
- 1/2 cup sugar, granulated
- 1/3 cup pear puree, pear jam or pear sauce
- 1 cup chopped walnuts
- 1 tsp. vanilla, pure
- 3 cups of oats

Instructions:

1. First, preheat your oven to 350 degrees F.

2. Heat brandy and water in microwave till hot, not yet boiling. Add the raisins to this bowl. Leave in oven so they can soak.

3. Combine salt, cinnamon, baking soda and flour in medium sized bowl.

4. Beat butter in large sized bowl with electric mixer, till it is fluffy. Add the sugars while mixing at med. speed till mixture is creamy. Then add vanilla and eggs. Combine well.

5. Remove the raisins from water and brandy mixture. Allow to drain in sink over fine strainer.

6. Add the flour combination mixture and combine well. Stir in drained raisins, oats and walnuts and mix thoroughly.

7. Drop 2-tbsp.-sized round dough balls on ungreased cookie sheets. Bake till just lightly browned.

8. Remove cookie sheet from the oven. Allow to cool for a few minutes. Remove the cookies onto wire rack. Serve when you desire.

OOOOOOOOOOOOOOOOOOOOOOOOOOOOOOOOOOOOOOOO

30 - Sour Cream Coffee Cake

These coffee cakes are so easy, they could even be one of your first dessert recipes to tackle. They have a different taste than typical coffee cakes, and it Makes them unique and special.

Serving Size: 9 Servings

Preparation Time: 1 1/4 hour

Ingredients:

For the coffee cake

- 1 cup of flour, all-purpose, sifted
- 1/2 tsp. of baking soda
- 1/4 tsp. of salt, iodized
- 1/2 stick of softened butter, unsalted
- 1/2 tsp. of baking powder
- 1/2 cup of sugar, granulated
- 1 egg, large
- 1/2 tsp. of vanilla extract, pure
- 1/2 cup of sour cream, regular

For the topping

- 1/3 cup of sugar, granulated
- 1/4 cup of sugar, dark brown, packed
- 1/2 tsp. of cinnamon, ground
- Optional: 1/2 cup of walnuts, chopped

Instructions:

1. Preheat oven to 350F. Grease 9-inch square baking pan.

2. Sift flour, salt, baking soda and baking powder together in medium sized bowl. Set it aside.

3. Cream sugar and butter together till fluffy and pale. Beat in vanilla and egg. Add sour cream.

4. Turn mixer to low. Gradually mix in flour. Stir till barely combined.

5. In another small sized bowl, combine nuts, sugar and cinnamon for topping.

6. Spread 1/2 batter in square baking pan. Spread by hand and cover bottom of pan fully. Sprinkle 1/2 of sugary topping on top. Spread the rest of the batter over sugary layer. Then sprinkle the rest of the sugary mixture on top.

7. Place in oven and bake for 35-40 minutes, till cake springs back if you touch it lightly. Serve.

OOOOOOOOOOOOOOOOOOOOOOOOOOOOOOOOOOOOOO

Conclusion

This San Francisco cookbook has shown you...

How to use different ingredients to affect unique California tastes in dishes both well-known and rare.

How can you include San Francisco recipes in your home repertoire?

You can...

- Make breakfasts like people enjoy on the West Coast of the United States. There are many different types of breakfast dishes made in the area.
- Learn to cook with fresh fruits, which are widely used in San Francisco.
- Enjoy making the delectable seafood dishes of California, including salmon, mackerel, clams, shrimp and cod. Fish is a mainstay in the region, and there are SO many ways to make it great.

- Make dishes using many types of available vegetables, which brighten up the flavor of San Francisco recipes.
- Make various types of pastries like coffee cake and blackberry scones that will tempt your family's sweet tooth.

Have fun experimenting! Enjoy the results!

OOOOOOOOOOOOOOOOOOOOOOOOOOOOOOOOOOOOOOOO

Author's Afterthoughts

Thanks ever so much to each of my cherished readers for investing the time to read this book!

I know you could have picked from many other books, but you chose this one. So, a big thanks for reading all the way to the end. If you enjoyed this book or received value from it, I'd like to ask you for a favor. Please take a few minutes to ***post an honest and heartfelt review on*** *Amazon.com*. Your support does make a difference and helps to benefit other people.

Thanks!

Julia Chiles

About the Author

Julia Chiles

(1951-present)

Julia received her culinary degree from Le Counte' School of Culinary Delights in Paris, France. She enjoyed cooking more than any of her former positions. She lived in Montgomery, Alabama most of her life. She married Roger

Chiles and moved with him to Paris as he pursued his career in journalism. During the time she was there, she joined several cooking groups to learn the French cuisine, which inspired her to attend school and become a great chef.

Julia has achieved many awards in the field of food preparation. She has taught at several different culinary schools. She is in high demand on the talk show circulation, sharing her knowledge and recipes. Julia's favorite pastime is learning new ways to cook old dishes.

Julia is now writing cookbooks to add to her long list of achievements. The present one consists of favorite recipes as well as a few culinary delights from other cultures. She expands everyone's expectations on how to achieve wonderful dishes and not spend a lot of money. Julia firmly believes a wonderful dish can be prepare out of common household staples.

If anyone is interested in collecting Julia's cookbooks, check out your local bookstores and online. They are a big seller whatever venue you choose to purchase from.

39704562R00063

Printed in Poland
by Amazon Fulfillment
Poland Sp. z o.o., Wrocław